BELONGING

BELONGING

A Lay Theology of Church Membership

BERNARD JONES

London
EPWORTH PRESS

The A. S. Peake Lecture 1973

Enquiries should be addressed to
The Methodist Publishing House
Wellington Road
Wimbledon
London SW19 8EU

Printed in Great Britain by
The Garden City Press Limited
Letchworth, Hertfordshire SG6 1JS

7612 0228 X

To
M
H *and* **C**
from whom I have
learnt so much
about
'belonging'.

Acknowledgments

GRATEFUL acknowledgment is made to the following publishers and authors for permission to quote from their works:

Allen and Unwin Limited: *Journeys in Belief*, ed. Bernard Dixon.

Cassell & Co. Ltd.: *Living Forwards*, Burnett James.

Collins Publishers: *Do We Need the Church?* Richard McBrien.

The Screwtape Letters, C. S. Lewis.

Epworth Press: *Ministry and Priesthood*, T. W. Manson.

Hodder and Stoughton Ltd.: *With Love to the Church*, Monica Furlong.

Jesus People Speak out, Ruben Ortega.

Macmillan Ltd.: *Underneath the Water*, Charles Causley.

John Murray Ltd.: *Collected Poems*, John Betjeman.

S.C.M. Press Ltd.: *Dogmatics in Outline*, Karl Barth.

Secular Evangelism, Fred Brown.

New Delhi Speaks,

The Jesus Kids, Roger Palms.

Letters and Papers, Dietrich Bonhoeffer.

The Layman in Christian History, ed. Neill and Weber.

Sometimes I weep, Ken Walsh.

Faith of the People of God, John Macquarrie.

Search Press, *The Church*, Hans Küng.

Westminster Press, Philadelphia: *These Found the Way*, ed. D. W. Soper.

The Registrars of the Convocations of Canterbury and York, *Revised Confirmation Service*.

The United Reformed Church, *Belonging to the Church*.

To the Reverend Philip Spence, who readily co-operated in illustrating the text with his cartoons, and to the Reverend Graham Jeffery for permission to use cartoons from *More Barnabas*, published by Wolfe Publishing Ltd., the author expresses his sincere thanks.

Contents

Introduction

A MINISTER was visiting a child from the church who was in hospital and was somewhat taken aback, but delighted, when the little boy greeted him, 'Hello, you work at *my* church don't you?' The little boy couldn't explain it but he knew they both *belonged*.

These pages are written to explore what belonging means for the ordinary church member or would-be member. They are not for the man in the pew so much as for the man—or woman—in the house group, where so much lay theology is being worked out. This is not a record of discovery but a programme of exploration.

Arthur Samuel Peake, in whose memory the Peake lectureship was founded, called himself a high churchman. Although not ordained he shared in the training of generations of ministers at Hartley College, Manchester, but he always prized his status as a layman. He believed that any unbalanced exaltation of the ministry would lead to the depression of the laity, the denial of the universal priesthood and the consequent depreciation of the Church as a whole. This was the sense in which he was a high churchman—the Church consists of Jesus Christ and the members of his body. Peake had a doctrine of the ministry, but we are concerned with the theology of church membership—the theology of belonging—and no topic could more appropriately be the subject of a Peake lecture.

The author is not a layman in the generally accepted sense, but in so far as the laity is the whole people of God he claims to be a layman as well as a minister. In the same way every layman belongs to the priesthood of all believers and must share in the ministry of the people of God.

1. We're marching to Zion

We're marching to Zion,
Beautiful, beautiful Zion,
We're marching upward to Zion,
The beautiful City of God.

THE CHAPEL stood on a hill overlooking Liverpool's dockland. We children embarked on the twenty-minute walk at least twice each Sunday. Appropriately enough we walked up Beacon Lane and finally arrived at the chapel, called Zion. We thought the hymn had been specially written for us; it was an upward march to Zion.

It was not a beautiful building. The nineteenth-century architect had neither the vision nor the resources that enabled twentieth-century architects to adorn Liverpool's hilltops with twin Cathedrals. The architecture might be described as 'double-storey dog-kennel'. In the semi-basement was the Sunday School. There they told us the stories of Jesus and gave us tea parties. Heaven will be something of a disappointment if there are not long trestle tables with tea-urns at the end and thick pink-rimmed crockery with 'Zion' printed on the side, for did we not ask God to be present at *our* table and in return we would be asked back to feast in Paradise with him?

Up the stairs, covered with coconut matting, was the Chapel. It was no Laodicean institution, for by reason of the boiler at the back with a mysterious metal chimney disappearing through the roof it was always either hot or cold. The pulpit dominated the scene, with lights either side that came towards you if you screwed up your eyes during the prayers. Between the pulpit and the organ was a mysterious holy of holies covered by a curtain and during

Baptism means belonging

the hymns the head of the organ-blower bobbed up and down. But by the time I was old enough to enter this holy of holies enough money had been raised to purchase an electric blower. Above the pulpit was a scroll, which I had learned to read but could not understand,

O come
Let us
Warship
The Lord.

It was not written like that but that's how I read it. Sometimes there was a rustling of a sweet-bag in the pew behind and a peppermint cream was handed over to me. This made chapel worth while!

I could not know it at the time but I was learning experimentally (before the educationalists had thought of the word) the meaning of the One Holy Catholic and Apostolic Church. There were other churches, of course; we passed some on the way, but this was *our* chapel; we belonged. When you crept upstairs from Sunday School you were in the *holy* place, but anyone could come. Now and again my father or my grandfather preached, for they were 'locals'. (I only realized later that 'apostolic' implies passing on the faith from one generation to another.) Most exciting of all, we sometimes had 'missionaries' to talk to us who told us how our pennies from Zion could help to tell the stories of Jesus to children at the other side of the world. Years later I would study Theology and Ecclesiastical History, but my first lessons were learnt at Zion. Here I was baptized. Here I *belonged*.

There was a parable in the disappearance of that chapel. It was blitzed; the war damage compensation was used to build a new church in the suburbs. Now a new road is pushing its way through the site of that church and they will build again. The building has gone, the name has gone, but the Church goes on. As Isaac Watts put it,

> *Zion enjoys her Monarch's love,*
> *Secure against the threatening hour;*
> *None can her firm foundations move,*
> *Built on His faithfulness and power.*

Any study of the theology of Church Membership must begin with the local Church. Once the apostles had obeyed the marching orders of their Lord, it was no longer possible to join *the* Church. You could only join *the* Church at Joppa, *the* Church at Tarsus, *the* Church at Corinth, *the* Church where you happened to be. In these days of vast trading empires and take-over bids it is tempting to think that the Church is truly seen in the great ecumenical jamborees of the World Council of Churches or the lesser denominational world tea-parties.

However important these gatherings are, it is still impossible to join the One, Holy, Catholic and Apostolic Church. 'I believe in the Church, One, Holy, Catholic and Apostolic?' said William Temple, 'but I regret it nowhere exists.' You cannot join it but you can be baptized into the Body of Christ represented by a company of believers meeting in a particular place. Karl Barth said,

> 'Take good note that a parson who does not believe that in this congregation of his, including those men and women, old wives and children, Christ's congregation exists, does not believe at all in the existence of the Church'.[1]

This is why the school can never replace the church in religious education in its completeness. In the school children can learn about the Church, but only *in* the church can they learn what it means to belong.

Every local church has its failures; we can all criticize the particular local church. Converts who come into the life of a church may often be shocked at what they find, sometimes rightly so. C. S. Lewis's Senior Tempter, Screwtape, knew just how to exploit its weaknesses, when he wrote,

'One of our great allies at present is the Church itself. Do not misunderstand me. I do not mean the Church as we see her spread out through all time and space and rooted in eternity, terrible as an army with banners. That, I confess, is a spectacle which makes our boldest tempters uneasy. But fortunately it is quite invisible to these humans. All your patient sees is the half-finished, sham Gothic erection on the new building estate. When he goes inside, he sees the local grocer with rather an oily expression on his face bustling up to offer him one shiny little book containing a liturgy which neither of them understands, and one shabby little book containing corrupt texts of a number of religious lyrics, mostly bad, and in very small print. When he gets to his pew and looks round him he sees just that selection of his neighbours whom he has hitherto avoided. You want to lean pretty heavily on those neighbours. . . . Provided that any of those neighbours sing out of tune, or have boots that squeak, or double chins, or odd clothes, the patient will quite easily believe that their religion must therefore be somehow ridiculous.'[2]

No doubt Screwtape could have similarly exploited the weaknesses of the New Testament Churches at Corinth or Ephesus. The Elder John was well aware of the failings of the local churches. The early enthusiasm had gone at Ephesus; there was dangerous teaching at Pergamum; there was immorality at Thyatira, procrastination at Sardis, lack of fire at Laodicea.

Yet the Elder John also saw the strength of the local churches and if Screwtape had not realized the potential strength of the local church he would not have thought it necessary to give such warnings! The little company at Ephesus had opposed evil men. They had done a good job in the earlier days. For all their poverty the group of Christians at Smyrna was truly rich. The folk at Pergamum had stood out against persecution. The people at Thyatira were doing better than they had done at first. Even in Sardis there were a few people who had kept their faith. There was an open door of opportunity for the Christians at Philadelphia. And even if the door was closed at Laodicea, the Lord of the Church thought it worth while to knock. Christian devotion has treated those well-known words as addressed to the individual, but it is as well to remember that in the vision of John the Elder these words were addressed to a local church: 'Here I stand knocking at the door; if anyone hears my voice and opens the door, I will come in and sit down to supper with him and he with me'.[3]

One of the most popular games played by Christians in the last decade has been knocking the local church. 'I am tired', complained one church official recently, 'of people talking about the church as if it were a branch of the local Co-op, which must be closed the moment the sales decline.' We have had so many surveys and questionnaires asking people why they have given up attending Church. We have been reminded *ad nauseam* of dull services, dirty premises, poor preachers, increasing bus-fares and frequent migration. We are apt to forget that 95 per cent of the people who were coming last year are still attending this year.

In some surveys the researchers have had the good sense to ask why people still attend. While undoubtedly the persistence of a habit accounts for some, there are those who speak of their need of the fellowship, instruction, inspiration and support which the local church offers. 'I could never have got through the last few years,' said one member who had passed through a really difficult period, 'if it had not been for the folk at church.' A man, aged thirty-three, speaks of 'the fellowship of God and his people', and adds, 'Where this is lacking it is, of course, not a church. The true church is not just a building.' A woman of sixty appreciates 'the fellowship and blessing we receive, the feeling we are in the presence of God, and the friendliness between our members and the preachers'.[4]

Fred Brown, the Salvationist, who pulls no punches in his trenchant attack on the institutional church, is still ready to give three cheers for the local church.

'I resent the tendency in some quarters to ridicule the local church. In my experience the people who comprise such fellowships are the "salt of the earth". A minority of them, it's true, are petty and sometimes unworthy in other ways, but they are not typical, which explains why their antics are noteworthy in the first place. To suggest that most church members are a liability, standing in the way of the church's true mission and seeking to preserve old ways rather than face the challenge of the new is a travesty of the usual situation. They *are* the structures of the church, for they implement her policies, sustain her programme, and sacrifice for her cause. Without them there could be no resurrection or anything else.'[5]

It is as well to heed this word in these days of ecumenism and big deal reunions. Of course the local church has little meaning apart from the big church but the vast ecumenical empire would have no meaning at all were there not the local colonies.

I never realized when I was a small boy attending 'Zion' that the name meant 'City of God', but when I did learn that fact it became just a little easier to understand how the local church and the big church tie up with each other. There is a time for singing: 'Like a mighty army moves the Church of God', and there is a time for singing:

> *Not throned above the skies,*
> *Nor golden-walled afar,*
> *But where Christ's two or three*
> *In His Name gathered are,*
> *Be in the midst of them,*
> *God's own Jerusalem.*

NOTES
1. *Dogmatics in Outline*, S.C.M., 1960, p. 143.
2. *The Screwtape Letters*, Bles, 1942, pp. 15–16.
3. Revelation 3:20.
4. *Family Count*, Bernard E. Jones, Methodist Home Mission Department, p. 15.
5. *Secular Evangelism*, S.C.M., 1970, pp. 106–7.

2. Church membership in the New Testament

We realise that our Church must have a message for our own age and yet be loyal to the faith once for all delivered to the Saints.

—A. S. PEAKE

THE STRONGEST evidence for the genuineness of the New Testament Letters is found in the pictures given of the local churches. There is no attempt to gloss over their imperfections; the portraits of the early Christians are painted warts and all. They broke up into cliques at Corinth; they sued one another in the courts; they sponged on one another at Thessalonica; they were greedy and selfish; there were distinctions between social classes. These criticisms did not apply to all, but on the whole we are given a picture of a group of people far from perfect, yet who knew they were 'called to be saints'. They knew that they belonged to something more than a religious club, and Paul and others who addressed letters to the young churches were never tired of reminding them that they belonged to something big.

The church in the New Testament is described in many ways. The Church is the Bride of Christ, the Body of Christ, a holy priesthood, the new Jerusalem, to mention but a few of the images used.

Chiefly the Church was described as the people of God. Paul writes in the letter to the Romans recalling the promise made to Israel through Hosea, 'Those who are not my people I will call My People'.[1] In the first letter of Peter we read,

'You are a chosen race, a royal priesthood, a dedicated nation, and a people claimed by God for his own, to proclaim the triumph of him who has called you out of darkness into his marvellous light. You are now the people of God, who once were not his people.'[2]

When Israel is described as 'a people' it is relatively easy to understand how an individual becomes a member, 'a son of Israel'. He is born into Israel; if a male he is circumcized and shares in the covenant made with Abraham. In the history of Israel the prophets had constantly warned against the danger of trusting to outward belonging. They had been told of the new covenant written in the heart; they had been told to rend their hearts and not their garments. John the Baptist had warned his listeners against depending upon their Jewish birthright. If all that was required was a plentiful supply of sons of Abraham, God could provide as many as were needed. Baptism had been used before the time of John as a sign that a gentile had become a Jew by faith. John invited the Jews themselves to become real Jews inwardly as well as outwardly. John's baptism was the sign of a new beginning—Jews by birth were becoming 'sons of Abraham' in the spirit. In the same way Zacchaeus was declared to be a 'son of Abraham' when he acted like a true member of the people of God.

The Baptism of the early Church was a sign that individuals were being incorporated into the people of God. They were becoming 'laymen,' members of the *Laos Theou*—the people of God. A layman has come to be thought of as a non-professional Christian, when his title really means that he is one of the people of God. Ministers and other members of the church are 'laymen' in this sense, and while we need a name to distinguish those who have not been ordained it is a pity that the word 'layman' has been so used.

Because the people of God were always associated with the City of God, typified by Jerusalem, the church was understandably described as the City of God in the book of Revelation as well as in the letters to the Hebrews and the Galatians. For the Christians this City was not to be identified with any earthly Jerusalem. The Holy City, the new Jerusalem, comes down out of heaven like a bride adorned for her husband. It comes because God has his dwelling among men. 'He will dwell among them and they shall be *his people.*'[3] Just as Mount Sinai was the symbol of the presence of God to his people in the Old Testament, so Christians were reminded of the new Mount Zion. 'You stand before Mount Zion and the city of the living God, heavenly Jerusalem, before myriads of angels, the full concourse and assembly of the first-born citizens of heaven.'[4]

The Jews were not the people of God simply because they were Jews but because of the Covenant made with Abraham, and we shall not understand what the early Christians had to say about the Church unless we understand it as the people of God, bound to him by Covenant relationship, and Jesus as the mediator of the New Covenant. Indeed we have lost something by the traditional use of the word 'Testament' to describe the two parts of the Bible, which is quite simply a book about the Old Covenant and the New Covenant. The New Testament is the book about the establishment of the Church by the New Covenant.

As the Christians moved out from the environment of Jewish thought, they entered the world of the Roman Empire. Paul was all along familiar with the two backgrounds. It became natural to think of the local churches as colonies of the City of God. There were so many parallels between the Church and the Empire. 'Caesar is Lord' was one of the battle cries of the Empire; the Christians looked for the time when every knee would bow at the name of Jesus and every tongue confess 'Jesus Christ is Lord'. Wherever the Roman Citizen went he retained his citizenship; the Christians were reminded that wherever they were they were not strangers or foreigners but fellow-citizens with the saints. The Roman soldier took his oath of loyalty—his *sacramentum*—before he went on campaign; the Christian shared in the two *sacramenta* of Baptism and Holy Communion. If the Roman soldier travelled across the world, inspired by the banner of Rome, inscribed with the letters SPQR, the Christian travelled across the world on the strength of the promise that the Lord of the Church would be with his people to the end of time.

If the Church is described as the New Israel, it is also described as the New Creation. 'When anyone is united to Christ there is a new world; the old order has gone, and a new order has already begun.'[5] The Christians at Ephesus were told, 'You must be made new in mind and spirit, and put on the new nature of God's creating, which shows itself in the just and devout life called for by the truth.'[6]

A member of the Church was someone who had been united to Christ and was part of the new creation. Indeed he was part of the new humanity. This may appear to be a very sophisticated metaphysical statement, yet when Paul wished to add emphasis to his advice to the Colossian people to give up telling lies, he put it this way:

'Stop lying to one another, now that you have discarded the old nature with its deeds and have put on the new nature, which is being constantly renewed in the image of its Creator and brought to know God. There is no question here of Greek and Jew, circumcized and un-circumcized, barbarian, Scythian, slave and freeman but Christ is all and in all.'[7]

It seems clear that Paul was saying to these far from perfect groups of converts, 'You are the new humanity, patterned on Christ'. They were indeed described as being 'in Christ' and Christ was in some sense 'in them'. This leads quite naturally to the thought that the church is the Body of Christ. When I think of my hand, for instance, it is perfectly clear that I am *in* my hand when I write or when I shake hands, and it is equally clear that my hand is part of me. This is of course what the word 'member' means. Only a living organism can have 'members' or 'limbs'. To talk of being a member of a computer is nonsense.

We must guard ourselves against thinking that Paul always means the same thing when he uses the phrase 'the Body of Christ'. It is after all a figure of speech. The central passage is in Romans, chapters 5:8. Becoming a member of the body of Christ is contrasted with belonging to a dead body. Union with Christ offers a resurrection. A Christian is no longer to be thought of as 'in Adam' but 'in Christ'. Whatever interpretation was given to baptism in the early days of the Church, Paul gave it a new or fuller meaning when he described the going down into the water as dying with Christ and rising from the water as coming to life in Christ.

'Have you forgotten,' wrote Paul, 'that when we were baptized into union with Christ Jesus we were baptized into his death? By baptism we were buried with him, and lay dead, in order that, as Christ was raised from the dead in the splendour of the Father, so also we might set our feet upon the new path of life.'[8]

That new path of life was membership of the Church. They were incorporated into Christ; they were brought *in corpore* —into the body of Christ.

When Paul wrote to the Church at Corinth, reminding them that they were members of the Body of Christ, he was dealing with a particular situation. The Spirit seemed to be manifesting himself in many different ways, and the thought of the different functions of the members of the body was an obvious illustration. After using this illustration in a general way, Paul sums it all up by saying, 'Now you are Christ's body, and each of you a limb or organ of it'.[9]

He wrote a similar message to the Christians at Rome, and to the Christians at Ephesus he wrote words which seem to sum up his teaching about the unity of the Church,

'There is one body and one Spirit, as there is also one hope held out in God's call to you; one Lord, one Faith, one baptism; one God and Father of all, who is over all and through all and in all.'[10]

When we ask what it is that binds the Church together, the unity is expressed in various ways.

'It is from the Head that the whole body with all its joints and ligaments, receives its supplies, and thus knit together grows according to God's design.'[11]

At the same time it is the Spirit who gives life to the body, just as the Spirit breathed life into the first Adam.

'Indeed we were all brought into one body by baptism, in the one Spirit . . . and that one Holy Spirit was poured out for us all to drink.'[12]

In the chapter that follows Paul points out that Love is the greatest gift of the Spirit and this gives unity to the whole body. He urges the Ephesians to 'make fast with bonds of peace the unity which the Spirit gives'.[13] Again it should be noted that the word translated 'bonds' means also 'ligaments'—that which holds the body together.

From all that has been said it is clear that the church was not an organization that an individual went along to join as he might make an application to join a golf club. It was an 'ecclesia'—a group of people 'called' to be 'saints'. Paul S. Minear tells us that there are no fewer than a hundred passages in eighteen different writings in which individual members of the Church are referred to as 'saints' or 'called to be saints'.[14] The Church was a fellowship of those who were being saved or who were becoming 'saints'. Unfortunately the word 'saint' in modern English suggests a medieval ascetic whose picture may appear haloed in a stained-glass window in the local parish church. The word 'hagios' means 'holy'. It is the word used to describe the Spirit—the Holy Spirit. The saints are those in whom the spirit of holiness is at work.

Many people who have never read the relevant passages in the New Testament have sung lustily,

> *From heaven He came and sought her*
> *To be His holy Bride.*

In the Book of Revelation the Church is described as the Bride of Christ, reflecting the Old Testament idea that God had betrothed Israel to him for ever. In the second letter to the Corinthians Paul reminded the members of the Church that they were betrothed to Christ, and elsewhere he uses the same analogy to describe the human relations between a man and his wife. The idea of a covenant between Christ and his Church is fundamental.

The one fact that most people know about the early Church is that there was an elementary form of Communism. 'They had all things in common.' They were a fellowship—but as with so many common words the meaning may become eroded. A fellowship may come in local circumstances to mean no more than a meeting of people who sit on fairly uncomfortable chairs from 8 to 9.15 each Thursday evening in an ill-lit room in the local church. But the fellowship of the early Church or the communion of saints was a way of life, sharing the teaching and the prayers, sharing in joys and sorrows, sharing in the witness of the Church in the world.

The Church is the whole people of God, in one sense called out of the world to be saints, in another sense called

SPENCE

Belonging means fellowship . . . 8–9.15 each Thursday

into the world to be the Body of Christ, to do his work, to speak his word and to be directed by his mind.

NOTES

1. Romans 9:25.
2. 1 Peter 2:9–10.
3. Revelation 21:2–3.
4. Hebrews 12:22–3.
5. 2 Corinthians 5:17.
6. Ephesians 4:23–4.
7. Colossians 3:9–11.
8. Romans 6:3–4.
9. Corinthians 12:27.
10. Ephesians 4:4–6.
11. Colossians 2:19.
12. 1 Corinthians 12:13.
13. Ephesians 4:3.
14. *Images of the Church in the New Testament*, Lutterworth, 1961, p. 136.

3. How do I get in?

The Church was locked, so I went to the incumbent—
the incumbent enjoying a supine incumbency—
'May I have the keys of the church, your incumbency?'
—JOHN BETJEMAN

M O S T of us have had the experience of walking round
from door to door of some country church, only to discover
that there is no way in for the casual wayfarer. Getting into
the Church in New Testament times was not a matter of
finding the right door; there was no door and no building.
The Gospel was preached; the hearers were called to repentance and to receive the gift of the Holy Spirit; those who
responded were baptized; they were then members of the
fellowship, receiving instruction from the apostles, sharing in
the prayers and breaking bread together.

There is a similar pattern throughout the New Testament.
Philip told the Ethiopian eunuch the good news about
Jesus; he accepted this good news as applying to him and
was baptized. In the case of Saul of Tarsus Jesus confronted
him on the Damascus road; Ananias laid hands on him so
that he should receive his sight and be filled with the Holy
Spirit; then Saul was baptized. Baptism was the sign and
seal of membership of the Body of Christ. 'Indeed, we were
all brought into one body by baptism, in the one Spirit.'[1]
It would be wrong, of course, to isolate baptism, the outward sign, from the attendant experience of repentance, the
declaration of one's faith and the gift of the Holy Spirit. In
the mind of the New Testament writers the outward sign
and the inward renewal were inseparably connected.

One can see the logic that led the early Church to adopt
the practice of infant baptism. If the Church is the new

May I have the keys of the church, your incumbency?

Israel, the people of God, then Baptism is the sign of the new covenant relationship, and if Jewish children could be incorporated into the people of God by circumcision then the children of Christian parents could be incorporated into the new Israel by baptism. But this was to do just what the New Testament writers avoided; the outward act and the inward renewal were separated.

A new theology of baptism was required. A new-born child could not understand the good news of Jesus; he could not repent; he could not affirm his faith; he could not show any of the usual signs of having received the gift of the Holy Spirit.

Then what happens to a child in baptism? According to traditional Roman Catholic teaching it effects the remission of all sin, original and actual, but it lacks the completeness which is given at confirmation when the Holy Spirit is conferred by anointing with oil and the laying on of the bishop's hands. Infants may be confirmed at baptism but it is usually deferred until the age of seven or so. Luther held that regeneration takes place at baptism. Calvin held that children cannot have an adult faith. 'Children', he writes, are 'baptised for future repentance and faith. Though these are not yet formed in them, the seed of both lies hid in them by the secret operation of the Spirit.'[2]

The traditional position of the Anglican Church is expressed in the Article which declares, 'Baptism is a sign of regeneration or new birth whereby, as by an instrument, they that receive baptism rightly are grafted into the Church: the promise of the forgiveness of sin, and of our adoption to be the sons of God by the Holy Ghost are visibly signed and sealed.'

However neatly the theologians may argue the point, one of the results of the practice of infant baptism has been to surround it with the aura of magic and superstition. It is little wonder that the Baptists reaffirmed the connection between baptism and confession of faith and sins, and saw it as a response to the preaching of the word.[3] There is a growing body of opinion in all the churches that baptism should be a rite for believers, not to be imposed upon children by their parents.

Many, however, still see in infant baptism a valid initiation into the Christian life. The Church is declaring that the Gospel is true for this particular child. The parents and the local church accept the responsibility of making the Gospel clear to the child as he grows towards maturity. Prayer for the Holy Spirit is offered. It is fitting, some argue, that baptism should take place when we can know nothing about it as this symbolizes the truth that we are saved not by any decision of our own but by the free grace of God.

The Roman Catholic Church declares that a baptized child is a member as does the Anglican Church. The Church of Scotland does so when the minister declares, 'According to Christ's commandment this child is now received into the membership of the Holy Catholic Church, and is engaged to confess the faith of Christ crucified, and to be His faithful soldier and servant unto his (or her) life's end.'[4] The United Reformed Church takes a similar position.

In the Methodist Church the child is received into the congregation of Christ's flock but the very fact that the term 'full membership' is used of adult members indicates that the baptized child is a member in some sense. At one period certain young people were recognized as Junior Members, and at present young people, 'when they sincerely desire to serve Jesus Christ, and are receiving regular instruction in the Bible and the Faith', may be recorded as 'Members in Training'. This has the virtue of recognizing that membership is a growing process.

All the churches that practise infant baptism would agree that the rite must be complemented by further teaching and nurture so that the child will eventually profess an adult

faith of which baptism is the promise. Those churches that
adopt the practice of dedication would also affirm that this
involves the parents and the church in the responsibility of
presenting the Gospel to the child in such a way that he will
be able to respond for himself at an appropriate age.

In what sense then can we say that the baptized child is
a member? On the analogy of the family he is a new member of the family. On the analogy of the state, he is a new
citizen. On the analogy of the army he is recruited but not
yet trained. On the analogy of the public school his name
has been put down but he has not yet passed the common
entrance examination. Some may prefer to use more am-
biguous phrases, claiming that baptized children are within
the *family* of the Church or within the *congregation* of
Christ's flock. Clearly where children are dedicated this
phraseology would be more appropriate. Where infant
baptism is practised it seems logical to claim that membership is conferred even if only in an embryonic form.

Perhaps the theologians are too meticulous in their
attempts to define what happens in infant baptism. At the
end of a baptismal service where the congregation is present
there is inevitably the circle of admiring adults and children
around the mother and baby. This is partly the expression
of the feeling of tenderness towards any tiny creature, but it
is one way of saying the baby now *belongs*. In some
churches this *belonging* is symbolized when the minister
carries the baby from the font into the midst of the congregation before he declares, 'We receive this child into the
congregation of Christ's flock'. If the parents themselves
are not members, then the baptism is the opportunity for
the Church to help them to grasp the meaning of belonging
and to show them that belonging is worth while.

The one interpretation that is foreign to modern man is
that by the act of baptism the child is more favoured by
God than the unbaptized and that the baptized child is 'safe'

should he die. Because this superstitious view is still widely held there are those who would like to abolish infant baptism. At least, they argue, parents should be given the alternative of a service of dedication. All would agree that the Church must give sound teaching on the meaning of baptism.

Broadly speaking there seem to be three views concerning Christian initiation which may be expressed briefly with the risk of over-simplification as follows.

(1) There are those who believe that baptism is a sacramental act which in itself admits the child to the membership of the Church; this initiation is complete in itself. As the seed planted at baptism grows the adult will recognize the reality of what God actually did for him at baptism. Confirmation may follow as a sacrament of growth but it is only a confirmation of something that has already happened.

(2) Others believe that in infant baptism the child is received into the Church but his membership needs the completion furnished by confirmation or confession of faith. He is a member in embryo but must grow towards the fullness of personal faith. On this view Confirmation is the postponed second part of baptism.

(3) Others again would prefer to reserve membership in its fullness for those who have confessed faith for themselves. They would claim that conversion is the true initiation. This view would be held by those who advocate believers' baptism, but there are others who would prefer not to use the term 'member' of baptized infants who cannot confess faith for themselves.

These three positions are not as opposed as they may seem to be at first sight. Those who hold that baptism is the real initiation must recognize the need for further instruction and, what are called in some churches, the sacraments of growth. Those who hold that conversion or the

declaration of faith is the real beginning must recognize the
value of the nurture and training in the Church and home
that often precede it.

What is certain is that the Church has an obligation to
help her people of all ages and at all stages to grow towards
mature manhood measured by nothing less than the full
stature of Christ. If the pattern set out in the New Testament is valid, then there must come at some time the
response of faith and self-commitment, and it could be
marked by confirmation, conversion or both.

In family life the child realizes day by day and year by
year what it means to belong to a family and there may be
special experiences such as illness, bereavement or a period
in hospital that lead to a new realization of what belonging
means. In the life of the Church the child should be led
to a gradual realization of what belonging means. In recent
years the Church has helped children to realize this sense of
belonging by bringing the Sunday School back into the
church. Too often the Sunday School fulfilled the function
of the Victorian Nanny, who had to look after the children
and keep them out of the way of the adult life of the home.
Now the child has the opportunity of growing up in the
Church and feeling that he belongs from the earliest days.
Accompanying his parents to Holy Communion and becoming familiar with the church building all help. Providing
worship is not so obscure that he cannot understand anything, or so puerile that he will quickly spurn it, the child
will grow towards the fullness of membership quite
naturally.

Thought is being given in some of the churches to the
possibility of making the first communion and subsequent
attendance part of the growing process.[5] There must be
many children, who have accompanied their parents to the
communion rail, who reach a stage described by Dr John
Robinson. 'They were not nearly ready for Confirmation

．．

but they were ready for Communion. "Mummy, it would help if I could have the bread and wine too." [6] This, of course, would take something away from confirmation, but it might also add something to it. Confirmation would no longer be seen as providing a life member's ticket for Holy Communion, but would be seen as the adult acceptance of the full responsibilities of membership of the Church. Confirmation, in this view, would be deferred until the individual had reached a further point of commitment, when he would be more able to enter into the promises involved with heart and mind.

Some have argued for an earlier confirmation, but confirmation has too frequently been seen as a kind of 'leaving certificate'. So many who are confirmed at an early age are not seen in church very much after the age of fifteen. This can only cheapen confirmation. It may be far better to have fewer full members deeply involved in the life of the church than a vast army of deserters.

If confirmation were thus deferred to a later stage, then it might be that membership would take on again something of its New Testament meaning. When a person had reached a point where he was ready to confess his faith and to accept the full obligations of membership, then he would signify this by becoming a member through confirmation or, if not already baptized, through baptism.

NOTES
1. Corinthians 12:13.
2. Institutes, **Book IV, Ch. XVI, 19–20.**
3. Baptist Confession, Amsterdam, 1611, **Article XIII.**
4. Book of Common Order.
5. *Christian Initiation*, 1971, popularly known as the Ely Report. The subject is also under discussion in the Methodist Church.
6. *Meeting, Membership and Ministry*, John Robinson, Prism Pamphlet No. 31, 1966.

4. See how they grow

I want always to be a little boy and have fun.
—PETER PAN

When I grew up I had finished with childish things.
—ST PAUL

IN PURSUING the idea of belonging as a growing relationship it may be helpful to look at another realm of human experience. Burnett James, a cripple confined to a wheelchair, described what can only be called a conversion to music in this way.

'One night, in the winter of 1938-9, I was granted insight into the meaning of music as revelation. It came at a point in a performance of the Leonora No. 3 Overture, conducted by Toscanini in the Queen's Hall—the trumpet call to be precise. It was one of the three or four great experiences of my life—something I can only call mystical penetration. The dramatic interruption of the trumpet, first from afar, then startlingly near at hand, cut through me like a sword. I was momentarily free from time and space. I entered another dimension. The whole world seemed changed . . . by the end of the performance, I was another man. . . . From that moment, music became the staff which put forth green shoots in my hands.'[1]

This story might be repeated by those who can point to one experience that provided the key to art, music, drama or poetry. In affairs of the heart some, like Dante, can describe how they fell in love at first sight.

Others, and there are certainly far more of them, would trace the progress of their musical appreciation through many slow stages. Some would be unable to recall a time when music was not taken for granted as part of the family background. Others would recall long painful hours of practice at the piano. Others would mention the many grades of musical achievement set out by the various boards of music. Some would name particular occasions which at the time brought the experience of music alive for them. Some would pay tribute to a particular teacher. Had William James set his mind to it he might well have written 'Varieties of Musical Experience' instead of his classic work on religion.

Religion however is more than an aesthetic experience such as that engendered by poetry or music. It is an experience that involves commitment to a way of life. Commitment is also a growing experience. The commitment of engagement leads to the deeper commitment of marriage and any married couple, providing they maintain their commitment, could testify to its changing nature. The commitment for better for worse, for richer for poorer, in sickness and in health, is not static.

A moment's thought about these human experiences will reveal the pointlessness of trying to force people into one pattern of experience. The automatic confirmation of young people at the age of seven or seventeen may or may not mark a point of real development. Conversion of the momentary type can be a transitory experience. Both confirmation and conversion have their place in the growing relationship with Christ and his Church, but the New Testament emphasis on growth towards maturity gives the key.

'So shall we all at last attain to the unity inherent in our faith and our knowledge of the Son of God—to mature manhood, measured by nothing less than the full stature of Christ. We are no longer to be children. . . . No, let us speak the truth in love; so shall we fully grow up into Christ. He is the head and on him the whole body depends. Bonded and knit together by every constituent joint, the whole frame grows through the due activity of each part, and builds itself up in love.'[2]

To press the analogy a little further, the hand is a member of the body from the moment the embryo is formed. When the child is born he can grasp with his hand but so many skills have still to be learned. The hand of the child who clumsily topples the pile of building bricks is just as much a member of his body as the hand of Yehudi Menuhin. This ability of the member to respond to the mind is not a matter of sudden attainment but physical growth accompanied by growing awareness and commitment to a particular task. In Paul's analogy it is the whole body that is growing towards maturity but this can only happen as the individual members grow towards Christian maturity.

For the child brought up in a Christian home the Christian life is a growing awareness and a growing commitment. This environment within which the child grows is provided by the Church and the home. In the revised Methodist service of Baptism the Minister says to the congregation,

'Members of the household of faith, who are now in Christ's name to receive these children, will you so maintain the common life of worship and service that they and all the children in your midst may *grow up in the knowledge and love of God and of his Son Jesus Christ our Lord*?'[3]

The parents are asked to respond to the following three questions.

'Will you provide for these your children a Christian home of love and faithfulness?

Will you help them by your words, prayers and example to renounce all evil and to put their trust in Jesus Christ their Saviour?

Will you encourage them to enter into the full membership of the Church, and to serve Christ in the world?'

The educationalists find it difficult to pinpoint the various stages through which a child passes in grasping concepts. It is certain however that within a few days of birth the child is beginning to understand the security afforded by the mother's love and care. This may well be his first intimation of religion. He will learn by natural experience and contrived experience. The whole process of education within church or school is a vast contrived experience, through which the child learns. But it will be so much conditioning or brainwashing unless he learns freedom. At this point the analogy breaks down. The hand must be allowed to decide whether it wishes to continue to grow within the framework of the Body. Confirmation is understood by some to be God's confirmation of his promises, but somewhere in the process of growth the individual must have the opportunity of declaring his own faith.

Dr Nels Ferre, an American theologian, described his own growth in the Christian life in this way.

'I have been converted three times; the first time to traditional Christianity; the second time, to honesty; the third time, to the love of God and man. And this is only the beginning of my conversion. . . .

I was twelve years old. . . . The midweek prayer group was small but dedicated. . . . As my father was picturing heaven, silently the deeper longing of my fuller self pressed tears out of my eyes, almost without my knowing it. . . . Suddenly torrents of words, long repressed, gushed forth and my heart grew light with joy. . . . The barriers between me and the group, and above all between me and God, were gone. I was forgiven by God and I belonged to the group. . . . Came the sciences, history, psychology, Biblical criticism, and a growing feeling that not every picture in the Bible, even of God, was respectably moral.... It was then that I became converted to honesty. By my bed I sank down, a weary college junior, and prayed, 'Oh, if there be anything to hear me, help me at least to be honest.'... My faith in the infallibility of the Bible, and my Christianity, disappeared together.... I picked at random from the library shelf *My Education and Religion* by George A. Gordon. Click! Came the light I needed. From then on I knew I could be both honest and a Christian.... Beyond the third conversion, however, there can be no step ahead except of the same kind. The third conversion was to the love of God, in thought and life; in the end that cannot fail, for firm is the promise, Love never fails, for love is of God and is God.'[4]

We may well ask at what point it would have been right to make him a member of the Church. It is clear that because of the environment provided by his parents he was already a member in some sense. There will be those who say he should have been made a member at twelve and others that he should have waited till he had passed through his doubts. Others again will claim that he had been a member all along. The important point is that membership is a constantly growing and changing relationship. Perhaps the Church has failed to show clearly that membership is not a status but a relationship, a growing relationship with Christ and his people.

A confirmation certificate must not be thought of as a kind of 'A' level certificate in the Christian faith. It is more like a passport for further travel. Confirmation must be seen as the initiation of a further stage of growth rather than as simply the completion of baptism. The Methodist Church renews this passport from time to time by issuing membership tickets. They may be thought by some to be a quaint survival from a former century but they serve as a reminder of the ongoing commitment of belonging to the people of God.

Paul reminded the members at Philippi that the Christian life is not an achieved status, but a pilgrimage.

'It is not to be thought that I have already achieved all this. I have not yet reached perfection, but I press on, hoping to take hold of that for which Christ once took hold of me. My friends, I do not reckon myself to have got hold of it yet. All I can say is this: forgetting what is behind me, and reaching out for that which lies ahead, I press towards the goal to win the prize which is God's call to the life above in Christ Jesus. . . . Let our conduct be consistent with the level we have already reached.'[5]

When Paul used the word 'perfection' it could well be rendered as 'maturity', a word used in a later verse. From the last verse in the passage quoted we can deduce that even in the school of Christ there are various 'levels' and the scholar's behaviour must be consistent with the level he's reached! Practice makes perfect. As Paul pointed out in the letter to the Ephesians already quoted, the whole purpose of the Church with its many and varied members is that all shall attain mature manhood, measured by the full stature of Christ.

The early Methodists may have something to teach us. For them membership was wholly associated with the Class Meeting. For historical reasons they were not concerned initially with the sacraments nor with the status of confirmed members. They were concerned to build each other up. The hymns of fellowship in the *Methodist Hymn Book* speak of this continuing task.

> *Help us to build each other up,*
> *Our little stock improve;*

Increase our faith, confirm our hope,
And perfect us in love.

Anyone who wished to become a member must have a sincere desire to 'flee from the wrath to come'. He would attend for a number of weeks. The class leader, unaware of the jargon of group dynamics but understanding something of human nature, saw how the new member reacted to others and how he progressed. If after three months or so he appeared to be a suitable candidate for membership, he was duly admitted and received the all important 'class ticket', renewable each quarter.

The old wording of the conditions of membership made it perfectly clear that the member was looking for something. It was not that he had necessarily found it, but he knew where to look. It was the class leader's duty to see that he did not give up the search and to encourage all the members to press on towards Christian perfection. This is in line with all that Paul has to say about membership.

If we can establish that a member is one who is on the way and who is growing within the fellowship of the Church, then the matter of when he is received as a member is relatively unimportant. What is vital is that the youngster should feel that he belongs at every point. In the development of young people the age of eleven or twelve seems to be crucial. This is why many people argue for confirmation at this age. Others point out that at this age the child is not ready for the commitment that full membership implies but that he might be ready, with suitable preparation, for his first communion. Confirmation and the assumption of constitutional voting rights would follow later.

So long as local churches remember the obligations accepted each time a child is baptized there seems little objection to controlled experiment. After all we are only trying to find out how best to maintain the common life of worship and service so that those baptized may *grow up in the knowledge and love of God and of his Son Jesus Christ our Lord.*

If it takes all sorts to make a world, it certainly takes all sorts to make a Church. It would be a great loss if the rich variety within the body of Christ were reduced to the drab uniformity of a multiple Church. Any attempts to get a standard confirmation age throughout the Christian world would be utterly pointless. Any campaign to insist that all Christians shall have passed through the same conversion experience would be ridiculous—as ridiculous as a body that is all thumbs!

If the Church is to be an effective instrument for the work of God there must be fully committed members. There will also be others who support the Church but do not wish to commit themselves fully. The true members are those who are growing within the body of Christ towards maturity, measured by nothing less than the full stature of Christ. Bonhoeffer was right. Only God knows who are members of the Church. All our membership statistics and confirmation returns may be aids to pastoral care and efficient organization, but we must not presume to number the redeemed.

NOTES
1. *Living Forwards*, Cassell, pp. 81–2.
2. Ephesians 4:13–16.
3. Italics mine.
4. *These found the Way*, ed. D. W. Soper, Westminster Press, Philadelphia, p. 131f.
5. Philippians 3:12–14, 16.

5. So what is a member?

We know what we belong to, where we come from, and where we're going. We may not know it with our brains, but we know it with our roots.
— NOEL COWARD (*This Happy Breed*)

THE TRUE members, we have said, are those who are growing within the Body of Christ towards maturity, measured by nothing less than the full stature of Christ. Some not on the official roll may be true members in this sense and *vice versa*. But the Church Council must make a decision at some point that such a person shall be received as a member or that such another person's name shall be crossed off the list. For practical purposes we must be more specific in our definition.

A church member confesses his faith and undertakes to act upon it. If his membership is a growing relationship with Christ then the faith he confesses will grow and change. How definite can we expect an adolescent to be? Can he, for instance, be expected to give assent to all the detailed articles of the historic creeds? It has been suggested that the Church ought to consider the total abolition of vows of any kind and accept instead an honest intention to live by the truth revealed in the life and person of Jesus Christ.[1] Whatever vows we ask young people to take they should be appropriate to the stage they have reached and there should always be the implication of a further goal.

The affirmations required in the three services we shall examine are fairly simple and direct, but there is still much for the leader of the preparation class to do. He must continually ask himself what the words used will mean experientially to the individual who will respond. He must not expect an adolescent to have an adult's grasp of the Christian faith, but he must be assured that confirmation will prove a growing point for the candidate.

In the revised Anglican service of Confirmation the Bishop says to the candidates:

> Those who are to be confirmed must affirm their allegiance to Christ and their rejection of all that is evil. Therefore I ask:
> Do you turn to Christ?
> *I turn to Christ.*
> Do you repent of your sins?
> *I repent of my sins.*
> Do you renounce evil?
> *I renounce evil.*

The Bishop shall then say to them,

> You have come here to be confirmed. You stand in the presence of God and his Church. You must now yourselves make the Christian profession in which you were baptized. Do you believe and trust in God the Father, who made the world?
> *I believe and trust in him.*

> Do you believe and trust in his son Jesus Christ, who redeemed mankind?
> *I believe and trust in him.*

> Do you believe and trust in his Holy Spirit, who sanctifies the people of God?
> *I believe and trust in him.*

In the Methodist Service, approved for experimental use in 1967, the minister says to those who are to be confirmed:

> 'Beloved in Christ, at your Baptism you were received into God's family the Church. You have grown in the

knowledge and love of your Lord. You have heard Christ saying to you, as he said to his first disciples, Follow me. You have already responded to his call, and you come now by your own choice publicly to renounce evil and profess your faith in him. You are now to be confirmed as members of a chosen race, a royal priesthood, a holy nation, God's own people, sent forth as Christ's servants and witnesses into the world. For all this God will strengthen you by his Holy Spirit.'

These words clearly recognize the developing nature of membership. From this wording it appears that full membership marks the point where a disciple becomes an apostle. The biblical description of the Church as 'a chosen race, a royal priesthood, a holy nation' makes it clear that the church the candidate is joining is not merely a local chapel or even a separate denomination. This is confirmed later in the service when the minister says,

We welcome you into the full membership of the Christian Church and the Society in this place.

The profession of faith is made in the following terms,

Minister   I ask you therefore:
Do you repent of your sins and renounce all evil?

Answer   With God's help, I do.

Minister   Do you trust in Jesus Christ as your Lord and Saviour?

Answer   I do.

Minister   Will you obey Christ and serve him in the world?

Answer   With His help, I will.

The United Reformed Church, which does not demand

uniformity in the service of Confirmation, has similar questions with the following direct statement as an alternative.

I confess my faith in one God, Father Son and Holy Spirit,
taking the Father to be my Father,
the Son to be my Saviour and Lord,
the Spirit to be my helper and guide.
I promise, in dependence on God's grace,
to be faithful, in private and public worship;
to live in the fellowship of the Church and to share in its work;
and to give and serve, as God enables me, for the advancement of His Kingdom throughout the world.
I promise, by that same grace, to follow Christ and to seek to do and to bear His will all the days of my life; and I trust in His mercy alone to bring me into the fullness of the life of the world to come.

In the Anglican service the Bishop represents the whole Church. In both the Methodist and United Reformed Churches the member has already been accepted by the Church Council or Church Meeting and is then publicly received. In the Methodist service the opportunity is given for a fellow member to welcome the new member with the right hand of fellowship. The new member is joining the royal priesthood of all believers and so is symbolically welcomed by a fellow believer.

One of the objections raised by some who prefer not to be committed to full membership is that they cannot give detailed affirmation to the credal statements of the Church. They want to be honest to themselves and open to new insights. The Church's record for honesty and openness through the centuries is not above reproach. The answer to this dilemma is not that the leader of the confirmation class should water down the traditional teaching of the Church but that he should expound it as a faith within which the Church has grown through the centuries and within which the individual Christian can grow. In the early days of the Church one of the simple affirmations of faith seems to have been 'Jesus Christ is Lord'. It is true that the responses required of confirmation candidates in the services we have examined are not quite as simple as this, but it should be made clear that the individual in joining the Church is not signing away his honesty or affirming a thousand and one metaphysical and theological statements. He is affirming his faith in God the Father, in Jesus as Lord and Saviour and in the Holy Spirit as Giver and Renewer of life. He is joining the people of God who in any age are called to be the people of God in the contemporary world.

When Simon Peter met Jesus he would have been completely baffled if someone had told him he was talking to the second Person of the Trinity. His knowledge of Jesus had to grow, and the theology of the Church grew out of the experience of Peter and others. This is only to repeat that confirmation, at whatever age it takes place, is just one further stage in growth. This is well illustrated by Hugh Montefiore's description of his conversion and subsequent confirmation:

'I saw in my soul One whom I instinctively knew to be Jesus Christ, full of light and power. . . . The experience meant so much more than the doctrine. . . . When the time came for me to be confirmed (after I had been baptized) I remember my tutor trying to explain to me about the pre-existence of Christ. I couldn't even understand what he was talking about.'[2]

Sadly enough, for many people the confirmation classes are the last occasions when they discuss religion seriously.

The duties of Church membership have similarly been

expressed in various ways. The Archbishops of the Church of England have set out the duties of members in this way,

To follow the example of Christ in home and daily life, and
To bear personal witness to Him.
To be regular in private prayer day by day.
To read the Bible carefully.
To come to church every Sunday.
To receive Holy Communion faithfully and regularly.
To give personal service to church, neighbours and community.
To give money for the work of parish and diocese, and for the work of the Church at home and overseas.
To uphold the standard of marriage entrusted by Christ to his Church.
To care that children are brought up to love and serve the Lord.

The following wording is printed on the Methodist Membership Ticket,

A short guide to Church Membership

All those who confess Jesus Christ
as Lord and Saviour and accept the obligation to serve Him in the life of the Church and the world
are welcome as full members of the Methodist Church.

IN THE CHURCH

A member is committed to Worship, Holy Communion, Fellowship and Service, Prayer and Bible Study, Responsible Giving.

IN THE WORLD

A member is committed to the working out of his faith

in daily life, the offering of personal service in the community,

the Christian use of his resources,

the support of the Church in its total world mission.

The Certificate of Membership of the United Reformed Church declares,

> A Church member enters into a covenant with God, the Father, the Son and the Holy Spirit, and with God's People.
>
> The covenant is to help and strengthen the Church member, and to encourage all God's people, as together they seek to discover His will and do it in the world.
>
> Membership means belonging, being part of the body of Christ, a member of it. It means regular sharing in worship, in Church Meeting, in witness. It means sharing of time, money and skills with the whole fellowship. It means being helped to be a Christian in the world, being numbered among the people of God.

The Anglican statement of the obligations of membership is an earlier statement. The more recent statements are not so specific in their demands. The prospective member may well question today as he might not have done twenty years ago whether belonging to the Church involves detailed obligations such as weekly attendance at church, unless he has made such rules for himself. The later statements are also more outward looking; the emphasis has shifted from personal devotion towards corporate witness.

Twentieth-century man is used to reading the small print in contracts and he may well hold back from joining the Church if he thinks he is committing himself to 'small print' obligations he cannot fulfil. The demands of Christian discipleship are heavy indeed but they must not be unnecessarily niggling.

Once a person has become a member the sacrament of the Lord's Supper becomes the continuing sign of belonging. Even if the member has participated earlier it will now take on a new meaning as a pledge of renewal. Where before it was a privilege now it is a privilege and an obligation. He renews the new covenant which he has specifically made in becoming a member.

For Methodists the annual Covenant Service provides such a renewal. It is significant that the branch of the Church in which the conversion experience was stressed, should also stress the need for regular renewal. The Church is seen as the Covenant people of God, and if the Covenant Service is understood rightly it is more than a personal rededication; it is a corporate renewal. The member is realizing again his membership of the people of God. The Covenant hymns written by Charles Wesley are never written in the first person singular; they are written for a covenant people meeting with their Covenant God.

> *He bids us build each other up;*
> *And, gathered into one,*
> *To our high calling's glorious hope*
> *We hand in hand go on.*

> *The gift which He on one bestows,*
> *We all delight to prove;*
> *The grace through every vessel flows*
> *In purest streams of love.*

Belonging is a developing process, an inter-action between those who belong to each other. There may be a point of initiation be it infant or believers' baptism. There may be points of growth marked by confirmation, conversion or some other experience. But membership can only really be understood as a growing relationship between the member, his fellow members and Jesus Christ, the head of the Body.

If membership is to be a growing relationship the Church must offer pastoral care and the environment within which that growth can take place. The Church must also recognize that an individual has a right in spite of baptism and confirmation to renounce his membership either formally or *de facto*. It must also face the problem of those who have the status of membership but who do not fulfil the requirements of belonging.

In the Roman Catholic and Anglican Churches a person becomes a member through baptism and confirmation. He may be on the pastoral roll or electoral roll of a particular church but his membership does not depend on that enrolment. Excommunication is used rarely and only for serious breaches of the standards of faith or morals.

In the Free Churches, which were either historically 'gathered' churches or took on that form, membership depends upon belonging to a local group, though baptism and confirmation are the recognized signs of membership. Most churches of this type will review the membership roll annually and the appropriate church council will revise the list. In earlier centuries the removal of a name would have implied excommunication. In the early days of Methodism such a member would no longer be eligible to attend the meetings of the Society. More recently the removal of a name has been simply a recognition that the member concerned had ceased to think of himself as a member, though a member might still be expelled on doctrinal or moral grounds. In most situations if a person whose name had been removed presented himself at a service of Holy Communion he would be welcomed and almost certainly his attendance would be regarded as some indication that he wished to resume membership.

An individual's membership is associated with a particular local church but he is a member of the whole church and within the Free Churches any transfer of membership is usually recognized with the proviso that the final decision rests with the local church. This means that every member belongs to a local church and can look to a local church for fellowship and pastoral care.

In these days of interdenominational co-operation and ecumenical ventures the question is being asked whether a person can belong to more than one denomination. If there is only One Holy Catholic and Apostolic Church the logic of it is that there is only one church for him to belong to. But until there is one visible church the problem is being solved locally in a variety of ways. There is mutual recognition of membership within one united church. In some churches all the new members become Anglican, Methodist and United Reformed all at once. In some churches a person just becomes a member of the local church for the time being and need not choose a denomination until the problem of transfer arises. These are makeshift arrangements until such time as 'all in each place who are baptized into Jesus Christ and confess him as Lord and Saviour are brought by the Holy Spirit into one fully committed fellowship'.[3] Some would like this mutual understanding to go further in recognizing that there are others such as Quakers and Salvationists who confess Jesus as Lord and Saviour who prefer not to use the outward sign of baptism.

NOTES
1. N. O. Porter in *Crisis for Confirmation,* ed. Michael Perry, S.C.M.
2. *Journeys in Belief*, ed. Bernard Nixon, Unwin, 1968, p. 180.
3. *New Delhi Speaks*, S.C.M., 1962, p. 55.

6. Well-wishers and others

*'Was he a church member?'... 'Well, no, not exactly,'
admitted Mrs Wiggs, reluctantly. But he was what you
might say a well-wisher.'*
— MRS WIGGS (*Mrs Wiggs of the Cabbage Patch*)

T H E   O N L Y   institution you can establish with well-wishers
is a wishing well. To build a Church a firmer commitment
is required.

Within the community of the Church there are in addition
to the many children and young people who are growing up
in the Church a considerable number of older people who
are not members. They are variously described as adherents,
non-members, or associates. It would be unfair to dismiss
them all as merely well-wishers. Many of them support the
Church in its various activities and often share fully in
the religious services as well as the social witness of the
Church.

There may be three reasons why they do not wish to be
members. First, they may think of confirmation as something for young people; they are too old for that sort of
thing. Second, they may take such a high view of membership that in honesty they don't want to commit themselves.
Third, they may simply wish to be associated with the
Women's Meeting or the Dramatic Society and prefer that
their commitment shall end there.

If confirmation is understood as we have described it,
then it can come at any age. A middle-aged man might not
feel comfortable attending the same preparation class as the
teenagers. His conception of membership will be entirely
different from theirs. The teenager may want to ask different
questions. There may be occasions when there might be a

The only institution you can establish with well-wishers is a wishing well

fruitful discussion between two such varied age groups, but the needs of the groups are very different. The commitment involved is very different. In small churches and sometimes in larger ones it may be that members will come into the church in ones and twos and need to be offered special pastoral attention.

The second group are those who do not think themselves worthy of becoming Church members, but within this group there will be two further groups. The one group see clearly the implications of Church membership, the commitment involved and the consequent stewardship of money, time and talents. They are at least honest in saying they can't take it. The other group may need the assurance that membership is not the mark of achievement but the mark of entering upon a new enterprise. Even some who are members have a similar attitude towards Holy Communion. 'I am not good enough.' The sacrament of Holy Communion is for sinners rather than saints. Chuch membership is for those who have started out on the way not for those who have arrived. But of course if a person doesn't intend to try to be a Christian then it is far better not to persuade him to become a member.

To the third group the Church offers friendship, a club, a place to meet, tea or coffee to drink. So many people are lonely that it would be wrong for the Church to turn a cold shoulder to those who need its friendship. There was a time when the Church thought of Youth Clubs, Badminton Clubs and such like as recruiting grounds.

'Come into my youth club,' said the parson to the spiv,
'I'll teach you table tennis and show you how to live.'

It may still happen that people come into Church organizations and realize that there's something there that meets their need, but if the Church is to be a church for others it must be prepared to offer men and women what they need with no strings attached.

From time to time the Church must say clearly what is is there for. We would be surprised if for a couple of years we attended a Conservative Party Whist Drive or a Labour Club and never heard mention of a political meeting or were not offered a pamphlet of some kind.

Within the organization we shall distinguish between committed members and others in that we shall expect committed members to take responsibility upon themselves in the way of stewardship; but we shall not make such demands on non-members unless they wish to be involved.

Should such adherents be invited to the sacrament of Holy Communion? If the sacrament of Holy Communion is accepted as one means whereby the young person can grow towards the full commitment of mature membership then it is clear that it can be a similar stage for the older person. Yet because the Christian covenant is implicit in the service it is quite reasonable that when the adult adherent has attended a few times he should be invited to take on the responsibilities of membership, but in such a way that he will not feel he is being forced into some kind of shotgun membership. Others will take the view that only members of the Church should be invited to share in Holy Communion.

Belonging to a church is very much like belonging to a family. It is not having all the names in the Family Bible that makes the family, nor is it the church roll that makes the church. Once the church is bigger than a family then we need some kind of register if we are to care for all the members who, unlike the family, do not live under the same roof.

There is bound to be a list of those on whom we can count to share in the work of the church. These are the full members of the Body. There will almost certainly be another list of those within the fellowship of the church, some who are growing towards full membership and others who are not members but who need what the Church offers. The Methodist Church has recently established a Community Roll in each local church, which includes all who are associated with the Church in any way.

If the church is a church for others then those who want the services of Martha will be as welcome as those who want to meet in the house-group with Mary. The Darby and Joan Club, the local authority youth club and the play school will be welcome. In a family the guest is made to feel at home and this is not necessarily helped by constant encouragement to 'make yourself at home'. The church must be by its very nature a place where people feel at ease, and if this happens it will not be surprising if they want to belong. Lest this last sentence should be misunderstood it should be added that the church ought at times to make us all feel desperately uncomfortable.

7. Do we need the Church?

Outside the Church there is no salvation.
—AUGUSTINE OF HIPPO

Jesus called the established church the synagogue of Satan. They are not of God. Because I went to church all my life and I never met Jesus.[1]
—CORNELIUS OF DALLAS

KATHY from Texas expressed another view of the Church.

'In a church I find the fellowship, and there I can hear the Word of God and I will admit there's hyprocrites in churches, but I myself have seen examples of hypocrisy in my own life and I try my best to work it out through Christ.'[2]

Kathy is a realist. The Church may be a poor sort of representation of the body of Christ, but is it as bad as Cornelius painted it? Jesus People are not alone in their criticisms of the Church. There are many others who would call themselves followers of Jesus who ask, 'Do we really need the institutional church in the modern world?' Among them are some of the people discussed in the previous chapter, who may offer limited support but do not wish to commit themselves to membership of the organization.

The Old Testament prophets asked pertinent questions about organized religion. John the Baptist challenged its presuppositions and Jesus himself put more than one question mark against the products of organized religion. There may be doubts as to precisely what Jesus said about building a church on Peter or Peter's faith, but no one would claim that Jesus envisaged the vast array of denominational empires spread across the world, owning between them property worth millions and having an army of full-time agents committed in principle to the spread of the Gospel and in practice too often to the maintenance of the institution. One can understand the protest of the Jesus Kids who ask, 'If the organized church is supposed to be the body of Christ, and if the church is alive, why isn't there more body movement?'[3] Organization has so often proved to have a deadening effect on revival. The Church appears to the Jesus Kids as a down-at-heel business being run by a skeleton staff, and they ask with Ezekiel, 'Can these bones live?'

James Kavanaugh, a former Roman Catholic priest, looked searchingly at what he described as his 'outdated church', and however much one allows for the angry young man syndrome there is still much food for thought. In writing the book he has broken what he calls 'the first commandment of every bishop—Thou shalt not rock the boat'.[4] Perhaps we have all been too much influenced by the symbolic ecumenical boat which appears to float so calmly at anchor on a smooth sea. Is Jesus asleep in the stern and have we forgotten the bits about launching out into the deep and Jesus awake in the storm?

Richard McBrien, another Roman Catholic, raises the question, Do we need the Church? in his book of that title. He calls for a Copernican revolution in our thinking about the Church.

> 'The Church is no longer to be conceived as the centre of God's plan of salvation. Not all men are called to membership in the Church, nor is such membership a sign of present salvation or a guarantee of future salvation. The central reality is not the Church but the Kingdom of God; not all men are called to the Church.'[5]

He goes on to say that the Church exists to work and

struggle and empty itself in the service of love. His conclusion is that we do not need what he calls the Ptolemaic
Church but we do need a Church that sees the Kingdom as
its goal and the human community as its place of operation.

If Augustine was right in saying that there is no salvation
outside the Church, then the aim of the Church must be to
bring every human soul into membership. This was not the
pattern given to the people of God in the Old Testament.
Israel—the people of God—was to be the suffering servant
through whom the world would learn of God. Israel was to
be the instrument of salvation—not a world power.

In the New Testament the Church is to be a city on a hill,
a light shining in the darkness, leaven in the lump. The
Church does not exist for its own sake but for the world.
The Kingdom is the end and the Church is the means. Of
course the Church needs more members, not for the sake
of prestige and power, not in order to produce more cheer-
ful statistics, but so that there can be more people sharing
in the work of the servant church.

In one sense the whole world community is the people
of God; it is his creation. Within the world community the
Church is the servant of God. The Church offers to the
community the way of renewal and the way to fullness of
life. The Church may be described as God's pressure group,
but it is not a pressure group seeking power for itself.
'The Church', said William Temple, 'exists for those outside it.' The leaven exists for the lump and eventually is
indistinguishable from it.

Bonhoeffer echoed William Temple when he wrote from
prison, 'The Church is only the Church when it exists for
others'.[6] Jesus was the Man for Others and so the Church,
his Body, must be the Church for others. Yet so often the
Church seems more concerned with perpetuating its own
existence than serving the community.

The Methodist Church began as a revival movement.

Buildings were erected to house the well-attended meetings. An organizational structure was created. During the two and a half centuries since the revival began the buildings have become more elaborate and the structure more complex. An attempt is being made at present to simplify the structure particularly in smaller churches, but a stranger who listens to the announcements in some churches might be forgiven if he gets the impression that the Church is an organization for running coffee mornings and committees.

Karl Barth likens the church that does not understand its mission to the snail that carries its little house on its back and just occasionally sticks out its feelers and thinks it has preached the gospel. The organization has become top-heavy. Such a large shell for such a small snail! 'Like a mighty tortoise moves the Church of God', parodied some young people.

This is the complaint that Jesus Kids make. One of them exclaimed, 'They go to church meetings, but you don't *go* to church—you *are* the Church if you know Jesus Christ.'[7] The young Christian probably didn't realize that he was only echoing what Karl Barth had said about a quarter of a century earlier. 'Today there is rather too much than too little said about the Church. There is something better. Let us *be* the Church.'[8]

The Church is described by some modern theologians as 'event'. It is something happening rather than an institution existing. The Church, they say, is best understood as a pilgrim people with no settled abiding place. The Jesus People show many signs of the New Testament Church—its strength and some of its weaknesses. The organization is kept at a minimum; they are not interested in capital assets; they claim to base their mission on the marching orders of Jesus rather than the standing orders of a conference.

The wise leaders of the Church, the responsible managing directors, utter words of warning. 'This sort of loose organization won't last. Look what happened to the early church. We've got to have organization; we must have order as well as faith.' Even John Robinson, who has done as much as anyone in Britain to rock the boat of the institutional church, declares in one of his most recent books,

'The inherited structure of the Church as a religious organization is one that we dare not neglect or despise if the Church is going to be an effective instrument for anything.'[9]

He also adds,

'As a bishop I have been and still am very much involved with organized religion. I can testify to the potential locked up in it. But I am equally concerned to unlock it. For it is a container, I suspect, in which those of the younger generation are going to be less and less attracted to invest either their faith or their hope or their charity.'[10]

There has always been a tension between those who have stressed the importance of the container and those who have treasured the contents. It has been so with the Bible. The Exile taught the people of Israel that they could have their religion without the splendour of the Temple ritual. They looked back to their days in the wilderness when God had been a fellow-traveller with them. When John the Elder described the incarnation he declared that God was a fellow-traveller once more; he had pitched his tent among men yet again.

The Christians learned to dispense with the Temple. Their great High Priest was on the journey with them. Just as the Passover was first a hurried meal for the people of God on a journey, so the bread could be broken at Emmaus or Ephesus, Corinth or Rome. It was John the Elder who pointed out that the local churches were in danger of becoming merely 'containers'; he described them as candlesticks. A candlestick without the candle is poor consolation in a power cut. It is possible to spend so much time in polishing the candlestick that we don't notice the candle's burnt out. The church at Ephesus received the blunt message that if they did not return to their early love then their candlestick would be removed.

John Robinson may be right in saying that the Church is a container with a lot of potential locked up in it, but others would ask if Jesus has escaped from the container, from the swaddling-clothes of the Church's creeds and the grave-bands of the institution. They could quote Charles Causley's *Ballad of the Bread Man*, in which he describes what happened to the young man who came offering bread to people who wanted cake.

> *They lifted the young man by the leg,*
> *They lifted him by the arm,*
> *They locked him in a cathedral*
> *In case he came to harm.*
>
> *They stored him safe as water*
> *Under seven rocks,*
> *One Sunday morning he burst out*
> *Like a jack-in-the-box.*[11]

Some would claim that this is precisely what has happened in the Jesus movement. The Lord of the Church has broken out of the church.

We must learn from the protests of the Jesus People and others. It may be that those who want to use the Church's material assets more imaginatively are right. A much simpler organization might serve the cause better. Yet through this much maligned institution people still find God. Within the complicated organization the real church is still to be found. Any local church may provide a mixed bunch like the folk at Corinth, but there is still a vast resource of devotion. There are urban churches whose members corporately and individually witness to Christ in the community; there are rural churches whose members are indeed the Body of Christ in the village. Monica Furlong made many criticisms of the Church in her book, *With Love to the Church*, but she also arrived at this conclusion.

'Within the strange, sprawling, quarrelling mass of the churches, with their stifling narrowness, their ignorance, their insensitivity, their stupidity. . . . I perceive another Church, one which really is Christ at work in the world. To this Church men seem to be admitted as much by a baptism of the heart as of the body, and they know more of intellectual charity, of vulnerability, of love, of joy, of peace, than most of the rest of us.'

And she adds,

'There are more people like this in the church than outsiders ever imagine.'[12]

One thing is certain; those who follow Jesus Christ can never be 'loners'. As John Wesley said, there is no such thing as solitary religion. To commit oneself to Christ is to commit oneself to community. This does not necessarily mean the institutional church as we know it. But community of some kind there will be and organization is inevitable. The human body only functions because it is an organism and the Body of Christ demands 'organization' however elementary. What we must guard against is perpetuating a vast organization from which the Lord of the Church has escaped or building a million memorials to a Lord who isn't dead.

NOTES
1. *The Jesus People speak out*, compiled by Ruben Ortega, Hodder and Stoughton, p. 30.

2. *The Jesus People speak out*, compiled by Ruben Ortega, Hodder and Stoughton, p. 30.
3. *The Jesus Kids*, Roger C. Palms, S.C.M., p. 57.
4. *A Modern Priest looks at his Outdated Church*, Hodder and Stoughton, p. 35.
5. *Do we need the Church?* Collins, pp. 14–15.
6. *Letters and Papers*, S.C.M., p. 382.
7. *The Jesus Kids*, p. 58.
8. *Dogmatics in Outline*, p. 141.
9. *The Difference in Being a Christian Today*, Fontana, p. 67.
10. *Ibid.* p. 68.
11. *Underneath the Water*, Charles Causley, Macmillan.
12. *With Love to the Church*, Hodder and Stoughton, p. 22.

8. Laymanship

A Layman is (a) a man who fits carpets.
         (b) a poultry farmer.
         (c) one of the people of God.

WHATEVER happens to buildings and investments we conclude that there is a future for the people of God, the *Laos Theou*, the laity. Numerous books have been written in written in recent years with titles such as, *To be a Layman*, *A Layman and his Church*, *A Layman Speaks*, or *Layman and Priest*. If Luther rediscovered the priesthood of all believers, then it can be claimed that the modern ecumenical movement has rediscovered the laymanship of all believers. Hendrik Kraemer, an authority on the subject, wrote,

> 'Never in church history since its initial period, has the role and responsibility of the laity in the church and world been a matter of so basic, systematic, comprehensive and intensive discussion as today.'[1]

Clement of Rome was the first Christian writer to use the term *lay man*. Up to that time the word had been used to distinguish the ordinary people from their leaders; it was the distinction between officers and men. It took on a new meaning for Christians. Baptism came to mean ordination to the laity. By the outward sign of baptism an individual's membership of the people of God was signed and sealed.

In the earlier centuries of the church the layman had played his part in numerous ways. Later the church became a clerical organization and the layman's role became that of

3—B • •

supporter of the clergy, a word derived from *cleros* meaning magistrate.

There was a lay revival at the time of the Reformation. The doctrine of the priesthood of all believers was re-discovered. In some of the Anabaptist movements the distinction between clergy and laity was abolished. Standards were set for the whole membership which had previously applied only to those in special orders; all were ordained to the royal priesthood.

In England during the past two centuries the lay revival has passed through three stages. The first was practical. Laymen shared in the work of the Methodist revival, not for theological reasons, but for the purely practical reason that the laymen were the only people available. The second stage was ecclesiastical, when laymen were fitted into the structure of the Church. In preaching, in the Sunday School and in church government, the layman began to find his place. The third stage is more theological. The layman no longer sees himself as a part-time minister or part-time church official, but as representing the people of God in the common life of the community.

An emphasis on the importance of the layman need not be accompanied by any anti-clerical feeling. It is rather a rediscovery of the nature of the Church as the Body of Christ. It enables us to see the ministry, the sacraments and the total organizational structure as means whereby the people of God can be the people of God.

The priesthood of all believers is not necessarily to be opposed to an ordained ministry, but it does asert that the high priestly office of Christ is shared by the whole people of God. The outline that follows was written by a distinguished contemporary scholar.

'The priesthood of all believers consists in the calling of the faithful to witness to God and his will before the

'Perhaps I had better explain this new scheme'

world, and to offer up their lives in the service of the
world. It is God who creates this priesthood and hence
creates fellowship among believers. Each one knows that
he appears before God on behalf of others, and knows
that others appear before God on his behalf. Each is responsible for his fellowmen, called to share in his struggles
and in his difficulties, called to bear his sins with him and
to stand by him in everything. The priesthood of all
believers is a fellowship in which each Christian, instead
of living for himself, lives before God for others and is in
turn supported by others: 'Bear one another's burdens,
and so fulfil the law of Christ'. The worship of this priesthood thus develops from being worship within the community to being worship within the everyday secular
world.[2]

Those are the words, not of a protestant, but of the
Roman Catholic theologian, Hans Küng. T. W. Manson
expressed the same truth in his Peake lecture some years ago.

'The high priestly work of Christ consists in his complete
oblation of himself in obedience and love to God and in
love and service of men. That work, decisively done on
the Cross, is continued by Christ in the Church.

The priesthood of believers means that they are per-
mitted and enabled to share in the continuing high priestly
work of Christ by offering themselves in love and
obedience to God and in love and service of men.'[3]

If we study these passages carefully we shall readily
recognize that the priesthood of all believers has much more
to do with our daily work, our politics and our home life
than with the question of who should preside at the Lord's
Supper.

If the New Testament pattern of the Church is to be
formative for us, then within the Body of Christ there will

be those who have special functions—apostles, healers, teachers and others, but all share in the common priesthood of all believers, who offer the world to God and God to the world. The layman as preacher, churchwarden, Sunday School teacher or steward, is given a particular function in the church, but his priesthood, though it may be expressed in these tasks, is not exhausted in their fulfilment. Nor is the minister's priesthood fulfilled when he presides at the Lord's Table. In Küng's words every believer must 'live before God for others'; in Manson's terminology he offers himself 'in love and obedience to God and in love and service of men'.

The Church must provide two kinds of training for laymen, (1) training for those with special functions in the church, and (2) training to enable all members 'to live before God for others'. Unfortunately there are those who think of Lay Training purely in terms of courses for preachers, teachers and church officials. Of course training is necessary for all such helpers just as training is necessary for the ordained ministry.

Prior to all such training we need what has been described by John MacQuarrie[4] as a Lay Theology. By this he doesn't mean a theology made easy nor a simplified or an abridged version of a professional theology, though he recognizes that it may incidentally dispense with some of the professional jargon. If the clergy and laity together form the whole people of God, then it is clear that the professional with his knowledge of the Word of God and the layman with his knowledge of the *World* of God must co-operate to discover what it means to be the people of God in the world. Theology is about the Word and the World. MacQuarrie puts it neatly when he says,

> 'Lay Theology is theology
> of the people of God,

> by the people of God,
> for the people of God.'[5]

Too often theology has been thought of as the exercise of professionals in faculties of theology and seminaries. The theology of St Paul was not revealed *in toto* on the Damascus road, nor was it thought out while he sat on a rock in the Arabian desert. It grew with his experience of the world. He knew that nothing could separate him from the love of God in Christ Jesus because he had learned it the hard way, not in a theological school, but on the highways and the high seas.

> 'Five times the Jews have given me the thirty-nine strokes; three times I have been beaten with rods; once I was stoned; three times I have been ship-wrecked, and for twenty-four hours was adrift on the open sea. I have been constantly on the road; I have met dangers from rivers, dangers from robbers, dangers from my fellow countrymen, dangers from foreigners, dangers in towns, dangers in the country, dangers at sea, dangers from false friends. I have toiled and drudged, I have often gone without sleep; hungry and thirsty, I have often gone fasting; and I have suffered from cold and exposure.'[6]

If a seminary is a place where seeds of thought are sown and grow then that is a fair description of Paul's seminary. To balance the picture one must recall his rabbinical training at Tarsus and Jerusalem. Ministers and laymen must *do* theology together. Neither have the monopoly of knowledge of what it means to be the people of God in the world; they need each other.

If Lay Training is confined to the production of a good supply of church officials who understand all about committees, amendments, points of order and substantive resolutions then indeed it will be a limiting and frustrating exercise. The little book, *The Layman and His Church*,[7] is such an outline for Anglicans. Other churches have similar booklets. It is obvious that someone has to know who has a right to be buried in a particular churchyard and what procedure is necessary if a clergyman wants to change his vesture! Useful as it is, it is not a book that will warm the heart of the church member who has just been received as one of the people of God. Too often membership has been seen as the key to holding office in the church. Involvement in church government and money raising efforts has sometimes so wearied members that when they have moved to another area they have resolved never to become involved again. The round of church meetings has become too trivial; the useless task too common; membership does not furnish all he ought to ask.

A lay theology, in the terms in which we have described it, would help to make sense of the organization, the money raising, the stoking of the boiler and the cleaning of the church. But once the theology has been lost or if it has never emerged, then the exercise is like cleaning and polishing a car from which someone has stolen the engine!

A lay theology will not only make sense of the activities within the church but will give point to our commerce with the world. At the back of our minds we still think that God prefers medieval architecture to modern factory design, that he is more interested in the thickness of the wafers used in Holy Communion than in the thickness of the tread on the tyres of the motorway transporters, that he enjoys Sundays more than Mondays. We have had some strange theology at times because we have made such a sharp demarcation between the sacred and the secular. The line is now blurred. We are urged to bring the world into the church and to take the Church into the world. This is a healthy reaction against a narrow pietism that saw the Church as the ark of the redeemed tossing on the troubled waters of the sinful world.

A lay theology—a theology worked out by those with knowledge of the Word and the world—may help us to ask the right questions and perhaps find some of the right answers. Sir Philip Sidney, who is remembered in British history as one who gave his bottle of water to another dying man, wrote of himself in one of his sonnets,

Poor layman I, for sacred rites unfit.

Yet in his dying action he displayed so clearly that sacred rites are not confined to the sanctuary, nor is theology.

NOTES
1. *The Layman in Christian History*, ed. Neill and Weber, S.C.M., p. 377.
2. *The Church*, Hans Küng, Burns and Oates, p. 381.
3. *Ministry and Priesthood, Christ's and ours*, T. W. Manson, Epworth, p. 70.
4. *The Faith of the People of God, A Lay Theology,* S.C.M.
5. *Op. Cit.*, pp. 5–6.
6. 2 Corinthians, 11, 24–7.
7. Michael Elliott-Binns, Church Information Office, 1970.

9. The Church in the Church

Why do we flee into our churches
Away from the world?
Closing the doors
And shutting the world out—
Why don't we open the doors
And let the world into our churches?[1]
—KEN WALSH

IN THE MINDS of many church members the Church is still the building. They think in terms of keeping the building going, raising funds for a new organ or being on the rota for the church cleaning. Many members think of their obligations as members almost entirely in terms of the individual. He must come to church, read his Bible, say his prayers and even if he doesn't do anything else he must give his collection!

How should a company of people who call themselves the Church set about *being* the Church in the contemporary world? How are the people of God to be the people of God?

In the earliest days of the Church they met to hear the teaching of the Apostles, to share the common life, to break bread and to pray. At the same time they ventured into the public world of the Temple and finally found their way into the wider world, into Judaea, Samaria and the distant parts of the world.

Through the ministry of Paul and the other apostles the Church became institutionalized. The unity of the scattered groups was preserved by personal contact and through letters. In such letters Paul reminded the scattered members more than once that they were all fellow-citizens and he described the local church as a colony. This is an interesting and illuminating analogy.

A Roman citizen derived his citizenship from Rome and he was still a citizen however far from Rome he might settle. The colony similarly derived its significance from Rome. Caesar had sent his forces into all the world to conquer in the name of the 'Senate and People of Rome'; the colony was part of the strategy. It was more than a little Rome away from Rome—it was a point of consolidation, a training ground and a pioneering community.

Just as the Roman soldier on solitary sentry duty belonged to the colony and at the same time represented the whole world empire, so the solitary Christian belongs to the colony of the local church and at the same time represents the whole people of God. The local church is not a kind of Scotsmen's club in New Zealand, a nostalgic gathering for those who want to sing the songs of the homeland and to escape for a while from the realities of a strange land. A local church is a true colony of the city of God in so far as it becomes a point of consolidation, a training ground and a pioneering community.

Let us pursue this analogy in more detail.

1. When a person becomes a member of the Church he becomes a fellow-citizen with the saints, a member of the household of God. He belongs to the One Holy Catholic and Apostolic Church, but he holds his citizenship in a particular colony, which only has significance because it is a *colony*. He will never make the mistake of thinking of the parish as his world.

2. If in any one area there are several colonies with different denominational labels the members must recognize that they are fellow-citizens belonging to the one commonwealth. Within the limits imposed by conscientious differences of conviction they must share the common obligations of common citizenship.

3. In some way the edicts of Caesar had to be transmitted to the local colony. The Word of God must be proclaimed in the local colony so that members and others may be reminded of their *raison d'être*. The Gospel does not change but our hearers do and the world does. The message must be given in the context of the contemporary world as a living word for modern man. The hints given by John Poulton in *A Today Sort of Evangelism* should be heeded. Of course the sermon should not be dull and we should use contemporary illustrations and assume a world background, but perhaps the most important point that he makes is that we should impart the *feel* of what we are saying. A sermon is not a lecture. Too often sermons are about tiny points of detail. These are not unimportant, but a congregation needs to see the large canvas of the campaign for the Kingdom if the details of day to day strategy are to be understood.

4. Because they belong not only to a people claimed by God for his own, but also to a royal priesthood, they will offer worship to God in response to His word. While the worship may take varying liturgical forms it must symbolise the offering demanded by Paul of the Christians at Rome:

'I implore you by God's mercy to offer your very selves to him: a living sacrifice, dedicated and fit for his acceptance, the worship offered by mind and heart.'[2]

The *sacramentum* of the Roman soldier was an oath of loyalty to Caesar. While the Christian sacraments must not be limited to this concept, the Christian, by baptism and participation in the Lord's Supper, is acknowledging the Lordship of Christ and pledging himself as his servant.

5. The local church will be a place where people can learn more of the Bible and the implications of the Christian faith for our own times. The traditional sermon may well at times give place to a specific teaching session, which may be Bible-based or community-based. We may begin with the

Bible and ask what it has to say to us about modern situations or we may begin with the contemporary situation and
ask what light the Bible and the Christian faith can throw
on it. In many churches no extra organization would be
needed to provide the teaching programme; people are
already meeting but not always purposefully.

6. The local church is a training ground and it undertakes,
as we have seen, to maintain the common life of worship
and service that all the children may grow up in the knowledge and love of God and of his Son Jesus Christ our Lord.
The majority of children in Britain are baptized. In England
and Wales the Methodist Church has access to one home in
every twenty where a child has been born. In total each
year the Methodist Church promises to maintain the common life of worship and service so that thirty-nine thousand
babies may grow up in the knowledge and love of God.
This is a big promise undertaken by the local colonies. If
we allow that growing up take at least fifteen years there
should be about six hundred thousand children and young
people somewhere between the font and the communion
table! There can be no more important task than caring for
the children growing up in the church and helping their
parents to fulfil their promises. Even if parents do not fulfil
the promises made, and even if children exercise the right
they have to choose for themselves and leave, the church
must not go back on its promises. The central departments
of the church can produce literature and advice but the
caring and the training can only take place in the local
church.

7. If the local church has a building of its own, then the
building itself must reflect as far as possible the ongoing life
of the Church. While we must not identify the Church with
the building people outside will make this identification
and the church premises must not detract from the mission
of the people of God. The stranger who had never seen

Rome no doubt judged it by the architecture and the customs of the colony. One who knows nothing of the Holy Catholic and Apostolic Church will judge it by the church on the street corner and the customs of the people who gather there.

8. Just as a colony had a strategy within the total empire, so a local church must devise a strategy. A stewardship campaign is such strategy. On the financial side it is a means of measuring the financial needs of the church against the financial resources of the members. But if this is all, it will achieve no more than tidying up the financial problems. A stewardship campaign should involve an assessment of the place and purpose of the church within the wider community and within the wider church. The total resources of the church and its members must be measured against the service that is to be rendered and the witness to be given. This is what it means to let the world set the agenda, just as the ancient world set the agenda for the Roman colony.

9. What is the place of the ordained minister in the strategy of the local church? He believes he is called by God to the work of the ministry and this call has been confirmed by the Church. He is a link-man with the wider church just as the layman is a link-man with the world. He will be a leader, enabler, initiator and reconciler within the local church, but not managing director. He is appointed to be shepherd of the flock, but this does not mean the members are to be sheep. The members share with him in the breaking of the bread, the preaching of the word and the care of souls; he must share with the members of their involvement in the world. In the Free Churches the minister will not be thought of as holding a priesthood differing from the priesthood of all believers. His authority is derived from his call, and the training given by the Church. The word minister originally meant 'servant'. We might get a little nearer to the New Testament understanding of the word

The minister is a 'care' taker

if we called the caretaker the minister, and the minister the *caretaker*, the one who takes special care within the household of God.

10. The Roman citizens were committed to the colony, to Rome and to Caesar. The member is committed to the local church, the One Holy Catholic and Apostolic Church and to Jesus Christ. God's business must be done in a business-like way and in the strategy of local church committees will have a place. A committee is a group of committed people and they should remember that the word *agenda* means 'things that ought to be done'; It has unfortunately come to mean 'things to be talked about'.

In the short guides to membership approved by the various churches the commitments of the member are listed implicitly or explicitly under the two headings, 'In the Church' and 'In the World'. This can only be a rough and ready distinction; the one doesn't make sense without the other. What went on in the Roman colony only made sense because it belonged to something bigger (the Empire) set in the context of something bigger still (the world). The local church only makes sense because it is part of the Holy Catholic and Apostolic Church which in turn lives its life in a world context.

NOTES
1. *Sometimes I weep*, Ken Walsh, S.C.M., p. 42.
2. Romans 12:1.

10. The Church in the world

It's not safe out there.
It's lonely—
There are many doubts out there,
One can't be so positive,
But there are people, out there,
And where people are,
God is.[1]

—KEN WALSH

'WHERE is the Church?' is a question that has been asked by many a visiting preacher walking or driving around a darkened suburb on a Sunday evening, and the few inhabitants abroad have not so much as heard of its existence. The preacher needs a map. Some maps distinguish between a church with a steeple and one with a tower. The mark on the map gives one answer to the question, 'Where is the Church on Sunday?' A cross marks the spot where the steeple people meet or where the tower power folk gather!

Where is the Church on Monday morning? To answer this we need a larger map. If we put crosses on the places where church members are working—offices, factories, shops, kitchens—we shall begin to get an answer to the question. To give a true picture the crosses should be put in for the members of all the other churches as well. On Monday mornings the Church is in the world.

So we could go on. Where is the Church between six and seven on Monday evenings? On to our map go the little crosses marking the homes where children on the baptismal roll are being put to bed, fathers and mothers are eating their evening meal and older children are at their homework. Where is the Church on Saturday afternoons? Where is the Church when there's a strike? Where is the Church when there's an election?

In the end the local church must have a global view for two reasons. First, it is God's world and God's people can never limit their vision to the local scene. John Wesley claimed the world as his parish. Second, God's Church is One, Holy, Catholic and Apostolic and the local colony of the Church cannot ignore the existence of other local colonies whether they be in the next street or the next continent.

On to our map must go the factories, offices, schools, colleges, hospitals, old people's homes, public houses, bingo halls and other places where people gather as well as the streets of ordinary residences. This marks out the immediate 'world' of the local church or churches. But there is a wider world and suburban churches in particular will be looking further afield to the inter-racial areas of the cities, to the under-privileged and other areas of special need. In the end the local church must take a global view of world need.

In the minutes of a long-closed theological college there is an entry for January 1870—'that a globe be purchased eighteen inches in diameter'. They were evidently encouraging the students to take a world view. Perhaps every local church should buy one and put it on the communion table by the cross so that it can be clear to all that when they come into church they do not leave the world behind. There could be no more appropriate place for it since it was at the supper table that Jesus prayed 'that they *all* may be one that the *world* may know'.

The Church, like its individual members, is to be in the world 'in love and obedience to God and in love and service of men'. This involves service and proclamation, two obligations that overlap and coalesce. Sometimes actions speak louder than words, but sometimes words clarify the meaning.

A member is part of the Church in the world; he can never be off duty as a Christian. George Macleod tells of an enthusiastic evangelist who asked a fellow traveller in the train, 'What do you do as a Christian?' only to receive the straightforward answer, 'I bake'. He was right and his wife at home might equally well have answered, 'I look after my family'. *Being* a Christian is the first obligation. A Christian doesn't spend his boss's time in talking about religion or typing out the church announcements. On the other hand it should not be possible for a man to work in a place for ten years without his colleagues ever knowing that he belongs to a church. A Christian must learn when to say the right word.

The same principle applies when the church member joints any other organization, a political party, a trade union, a gardeners' club or a dramatic society. He is not there to propagate the gospel but to make his contribution to the particular society. He may do more harm than good if he becomes a buttonholer, but again it does not mean that his lips are sealed.

The individual member, in common with other citizens, will take any opportunity that presents itself to offer personal service to the community, helping in the local hospital, visiting in an old people's home, delivering meals on wheels or offering similar service. We read in the New Testament that the Good Samaritan left two pence to cover bed and breakfast, not that he left a pamphlet on 'What a good Samaritan believes'! All that a Christian does should be guided by the mind of Christ, but he will not always wear his church member's hat. It is important that the Church should not claim so much of an individual member's time and talents that there is nothing left over for the service of the community or for the fulfilment of his personality in leisure pursuits. But wherever he is he is representing the Church because he *belongs* to the people of God.

Confusion arises sometimes because there are church members who specifically represent the Church in the world by reason of the office to which they are appointed. A diminutive boy saw the deaconess of ample proportions bearing down the narrow path to the little council house. 'Mum,' he shouted rushing inside, '*it's the Church.*' He was right. She was the Church. In this sense the minister, the deaconess, the class leader, the Sunday school teacher and others represent the church in an additional way. This of course only applies when they are fulfilling the task given them by the church. When the deaconess goes to the theatre, the minister to a football match or the class leader to his daily work, they are the Church in the world in the same sense in which all the other members are.

At times the local church must act corporately, as when a church or a group of churches establish a housing association. Or a church may corporately make representations to the local council on playing facilities for children. Again a church may provide facilities for a play group that is needed in the community but not provided by the authorities. In *Come Out the Wilderness* Bruce Kenrick describes how the church members in East Harlem came to the point when they must embark on political action. They decided that the Church must be in the world not just talk about being in the world.

At the national level the Church is in the world, represented sometimes by departments of the churches with special responsibility, sometimes by a President, Moderator or Bishop, sometimes by an individual church member who is an MP. At times prophetic voices will be heard, such as Trevor Huddleston's or Donald Soper's; at other times an ordinary church member will write to his MP or raise a matter in the correspondence column of the newspaper. All this is part of the Church's witness in the world.

We have to recognize that the people of God will not always be agreed on practical policy. This only serves to underline the plain truth that being the Church in the world is a very complicated business. Members of the Church need all the help that can be given to enable them to express love and obedience to God and love and service to men in their homes, in daily work, in leisure, in politics and in the total life of the world community. This help must come in a large measure from the local church augmented by industrial and lay training conferences. Minister and people share in the endeavour to discover how the Church is to live its life in the world. Like the Roman colony it has to become a point of consolidation, a training ground and a pioneering community.

Witness will similarly be a matter of individual and corporate responsibility. A local church newspaper can provide a vital line of communication with the local 'world'. A church magazine can be an instrument of evangelism but, like some religious people, it can also put off more people than it attracts. The physical appearance of the church is a silent witness every moment of the day. Sometimes a national or regional campaign can give impetus to the strategy of the local church, as can the mass media. The Church must be ready to use every modern means of communication. Yet as Karl Barth has reminded us it is more important to *be* the Church in the world rather than talk about it.

The command to go into all the world seemed so simple when we first heard it. Evangelism sounds so easy when you describe it as one beggar telling another beggar where he can get bread. Sometimes it is as simple as that, yet we must remember that the one who offered the bread added, 'This is my body broken for you'. It is no accident that

*The church must use every means of communication available in
the modern world*

the Church is called the body of Christ. The local church should be a place where you can get bread. If we have offered only bricks and mortar and membership of a religious club we have failed.

Belonging to the Church means that we have joined the people of God. We are called to be saints, called to grow towards the full stature of Christ. We are called to train within the Church for service in the world. We are called to offer love and obedience to God and love and service to men. Belonging can mean no less than this.

NOTE
1. *Sometimes I weep*, Ken Walsh, S.C.M., p. 39.

Further reading and discussion questions

1. We're marching to Zion

FURTHER READING
Secular Evangelism, Fred Brown, S.C.M., 1970.

BIBLE STUDY
Letters to local churches. Revelation, chapters 2 and 3.

DISCUSSION AND POSSIBLE ACTION
1. Let members of the group discuss how they first felt that they 'belonged' either in connection with a church they attended as children or the church attended now.

2. In the light of the discussion try to analyse what 'belonging' means.

3. Let two members write letters (before the meeting) recommending the programme of activities of your church (*a*) to a newcomer to the district who has been in membership with a local church elsewhere (*b*) to a new resident who has not to your knowledge had any connection before. Compare the two letters and discuss. Ought we to write such letters of welcome?

2. Church membership in the New Testament

FURTHER READING
Images of the Church in the New Testament, Paul S. Minear, Lutterworth, 1961.

BIBLE STUDY
Some sketches of the local church.

1 Corinthians 1:10–13; 6:1–11; 11:17–31.
The People of God: Romans 9:24–9; 1 Peter 2:9–10.
The City of God: Hebrews 12:22–9; Ephesians 2:19.
The New Creation: 2 Corinthians 5:17; Ephesians 4:23–4; Colossians 3:9–11.
The Body of Christ: Romans chapters 5–8; 12:3–5; Ephesians 4:3–6; Colossians 2:16–19; 1 Corinthians 12:12–31.
The Bride of Christ: Revelation 21:2–4; Ephesians 5:22–31.

DISCUSSION AND POSSIBLE ACTION

1. Which of the analogies do you find most helpful?

2. Examine some of the traditional hymns about the Church. Do the Bible passages throw light on their meaning?

3. Would it be helpful if a preacher were asked to expound some of the Bible passages at a meeting of the whole Church?

3. How do I get in?

FURTHER READING

Ye are Baptized, Lukas Vischer, W.C.C., 1964.
Baptism and Conversion, John Baillie, Oxford, 1964.

BIBLE STUDY

Baptism in the New Testament: Acts 9:5–17; Romans 6:1–11; 1 Corinthians 6:11; 12:13; Ephesians 4:4–6; Titus 3:5; 2 Peter 1:9.

DISCUSSION AND POSSIBLE ACTION

1. Invite a Baptist or a Roman Catholic to expound

their views on Baptism, or let members of the group come prepared to take up various positions in a role-play.

2. Discuss the advantages and disadvantages of confirmation at the ages of seven, twelve and seventeen.

3. Let members discuss their own confirmation and first communion and recall what it meant to them at the time.

4. How does your church care for baptized infants and parents? Have you read *Setting out together*, a wallet of leaflets to be handed to parents when the Baptismal Roll visit is made?

4. See how they grow

FURTHER READING
Journeys in Belief, ed. Bernard Dixon, Unwin, 1968.

BIBLE STUDY
Growing up: 1 Corinthians 13; Ephesians 4:13–24; Philippians 3:12–16.

DISCUSSION AND POSSIBLE ACTION
1. Is it true to say that Nels Ferre was converted three times?

2. What does it mean to love God with *heart*, *mind* and *strength*?

3. Does your church programme give real opportunities for growth at all stages?

5. So what is a member?

FURTHER READING
Joining the Church, A Manual of Membership, Epworth, 1968.
Crisis for Confirmation, ed. M. J. Perry, S.C.M., 1967.

BIBLE STUDY
The Christian Life: 1 John 4 7–21.

DISCUSSION AND POSSIBLE ACTION
1. Does the Church ask too much or too little of those who wish to become full members?

2. Subdivide the group to discuss the three short guides to membership. Share comments and criticism. Can you sum up the obligations of a member in one sentence?

3. How does your church care for members after they have been received? Try to recall the names of the new members received most recently.

6. Well-wishers and others

FURTHER READING
A Today Sort of Evangelism, John Poulton, Lutterworth, 1972.

BIBLE STUDY
Counting the cost of commitment: Luke 14:12–33.

DISCUSSION AND POSSIBLE ACTION
1. Is there a place in the Church for honest agnostics

who do not wish to commit themselves to credal statements they are not sure about?

2. Arrange a role-play between Mrs Smith, a member, Mrs Brown, who comes from the Women's Meeting, Mr Larkin, a member of the dramatic society and Mr Black who attends and does a lot for the church in a practical way but can't see the point of being a member. Mrs Smith tries to explain what being a member means and invites the others to think about it.

3. When would a non-member, perhaps a Sikh or a humanist, have the opportunity of hearing a fairly clear simple explanation of what the Christian faith means? Is there such an opportunity given from time to time in your area?

7. Do we need the Church?

FURTHER READING
The Difference in Being a Christian Today, John A. T. Robinson, Fontana, 1972.
The Jesus Kids, Roger C. Palms, S.C.M., 1971.

BIBLE STUDY
The Church begins to organize: Acts 6:1-7.
An Ecumenical Conference: Acts 15:1-29.

DISCUSSION AND POSSIBLE ACTION
1. Families don't have committees. Why can't the local church be just one big happy family?

2. The Church is not the building but how important is the building?

3. How can the members of a local church make sure
that they are always keeping first things first?

8. Laymanship

FURTHER READING
The Layman in Christian History, ed. Stephen Neill and
Hans Ruedi Weber, S.C.M., 1963.
Ministry and Priesthood, Christ's and Ours, T. W.
Manson, Epworth, 1958.

BIBLE STUDY
The great High Priest: Hebrews 10:5–25.
The Royal Priesthood: 1 Peter 2:4–10.

DISCUSSION AND POSSIBLE ACTION
1. Read the passages from Küng and Manson and let
each member of the group write down a sentence
beginning, 'The priesthood of all believers for me
means that. . . .' Discuss the sentences.

2. To test the claim that God speaks to us in secular
things let each member of the group say how he
thinks God has spoken today in his circumstances.

3. How can the Church help us to be better laymen? Be
specific.

9. The Church in the Church

FURTHER READING
Sometimes I weep, Ken Walsh, S.C.M.
The quotations at the beginning of chapters 9 and 10 are
taken from this book of prayers and meditations.

BIBLE STUDY

The living sacrifice to be offered by the priesthood of all believers: Romans 12.

DISCUSSION AND POSSIBLE ACTION

1. 'Forth in thy name, O Lord, I go
    My daily labour to pursue.'
    Let members of the group attempt to translate this poetry into prose. What should it mean?

2. Are there any ways in which the pattern of worship could be changed to make it more relevant to life? Hymns ... Prayers ... Thanksgiving ... Confession ... Intercession ... Petition ... Bible Reading ... Sermon ... Holy Communion ... the collection? (In discussing this question look ahead to question 3.)

3. Are there any ways in which the pattern of our daily life could be changed to make it more compatible with our worship?

4. Is the Lay Training programme of your church adequate? Are there ways in which you could co-operate with other churches for particular projects?

10. The Church in the world

FURTHER READING

Planning for Mission, ed. Thomas Wieser, Epworth.
Dialogue with the World, J. G. Davies, S.C.M.
God outside the Church, J. W. Stevenson, St Andrews Press.

BIBLE STUDY

Practical Living: The letter of James.

DISCUSSION AND POSSIBLE ACTION

1. Examine a map of the local area in the light of the first part of the chapter. Is your church 'on the map'?

2. A lot of church buildings have been closed in the last quarter century and they don't seem to have been missed very much. Would yours be missed?

3. "Is the freedom which the Gospel brings being sought and sometimes found outside a hide-bound church? Is God raising up faith outside the walls? Is he turning, as he has had to do many times, from the Church as an institution to whoever is willing to 'rise up and follow'?"—from the closing paragraph of *God outside the Church.*

4. Let each member write down a one-sentence definition of 'Evangelism'. Work towards a common agreement on what it is and ask if your church is doing it.